The Modern Investment Advisor

Table of Contents

1. Introduction

2. Building a Bulletproof Practice

3. What are affluent clients looking for in an advisor?

4. The "Ideal" Client

5. The Value Proposition

6. The First Meeting

7. Soft Skills

8. Technical Skills

9. Process Skills

10. The Sales Process

11. The Financial Planning Process

12. Fiduciary Duty versus Duty of Care

13. Building the Business

14. Practice Management

15. Building Trust

16. Relationship Management

17. Coaching

18. Entrepreneurial Approach to Time Management

19. Mental Health – Managing Stress and Anxiety

20. Conclusion

Introduction

Many books have already been written on what it takes to be an excellent investment advisor and what one can do to become better in this role. Very few focus on the advisor as a human being, the pressures that they are under, and the challenges they experience to help manage their own emotions and those of their clients. My first book "Sales Coaching in the Financial Services Industry" which was published this winter was targeted at sales managers in this industry. It focused on what managers could do to make the great leap from sales manager to sales coach, all with the goal of helping them to develop their people to produce even better results.

In my coaching practice, I work with sales managers, but I also work directly with advisors. The role of investment advisor has changed over the years and continues to evolve. Advisors are being asked by firms and regulators to do more for less, and in some cases with less support. Compliance with an ever-increasing regulatory environment of know your client, know your product, and transparency has put increasing pressure on firms and advisors – especially time pressure as it relates to advisors and their teams. These are all good things for clients, but they take resources, time, and money. This in turn places increased expectations on advisors to produce. Not only is competition fierce but more and more I find advisors expressing how overwhelmed they are feeling. They feel pressure to build a sustainable business and many struggle to find clients. They are challenged to differentiate themselves. Once they reach critical mass, they struggle to continue to add value and to retain these clients. They work for firms that want to maximize profit for shareholders. All of this while battling the headwinds of a mature industry experiencing declining margins and the disruption of technology. They struggle to achieve some semblance of work/life balance and to manage their time spent on work, home, family, community and personal growth. It can be very stressful.

So, it is with this in mind that I decided to write a book for advisors. One that contains ideas and suggestions that can help advisors to build a bulletproof practice - a practice that serves them and their clients well. I use the term "bulletproof" to describe a practice that attracts affluent clients and has minimal exposure to losing clients to another advisor.

Building a Bulletproof Practice

I think it is rare when they first get started for advisors to have a clear vision of what their practice will eventually look like. I know when I started in the industry as an advisor, I was focused on survival in the early going. I knew my salary would run out in a year and I would then be on straight commission. So, I had a year to build my practice up to where it provided a sustainable level of income.

Unless they are on salary or buy an existing book of clients, advisors face the same pressures today. Having said that, the more an advisor can begin with the end in mind the better. This can help them to determine how many clients they need and what their ideal client looks like.

I think it is important that advisors understand clearly what clients are looking for in their advisor. The easiest way to find that out is to ask the prospective client. A great question is "what do you like most about your current advisor?" Another is "what do you like that your last advisor did for you?" A third question could be "what didn't you like?" Once the advisor understands what the prospect is looking for, they can better determine whether they would be a good fit. I think assessing fit is too often overlooked.

What are Affluent Clients Looking for in Their Advisor

Matt Oechsli in his article "Why Financial Advisors Need These 3 Qualities" writes that advisors need:

1) Professional Knowledge
2) Empathy
3) Business Mindset

Clients today expect their advisor to be knowledgeable and qualified in their field. Most are looking for advice and as such are looking for an advisor who knows what they are doing. But they are looking for an advisor who also communicates well and who takes the time to get to know them. They really want to deal with someone they connect with on an emotional level. It is important for an advisor to approach their practice as a business. Just as an elected official needs sound policies and sound politics, an advisor needs to provide good advice but also do that in a profitable manner. Finally, advisors today need to learn how to cope with stress and to focus on controlling things within their control and accepting things that are out of their control. They need to be technically proficient. They need to have sound repeatable processes in place for acquiring and servicing clients.

In my mind, financial services will always be a relationship business. Yes, there are a minority of clients who have the time, the interest, and the knowledge to manage their own financial affairs. There are a few clients who may prefer interacting with a machine as opposed to interacting with another human being. Heck when I'm busy, and I have only a few easy to scan items, I actually prefer to use the automated checkout at the grocery store. But when I have a lot of items or when I have vegetables or fruits, or other items that require lookup, I will let the cashiers process my order. Many people don't like the experience of interacting with a machine and I think it will be some time (if ever) before automated intelligence can replace the experience of working with a top-notch advisor.

Advisors can be introverts or extroverts and most of us are a little of both. Those that are more introverted need to be able to "turn it on" when it is time to be in front of the prospect or client. To be really successful, though, I feel that advisors need to be good salespeople too. I believe in "salesperson DNA". Some have it and some don't. Top salespeople are comfortable having a conversation with a prospective client, they build trust quickly, and they are able to communicate effectively. They ask questions and are genuinely interested in helping the prospect. They listen actively and are able to determine what the client needs. They are able to explain complex concepts in simple terms.

Advisors need strong technical skills too, but many of these can be learned. I can teach someone to become a strong financial planner. They can learn tax rules and how their clients can minimize and defer income tax. They can even learn how to operate planning software.

A business mindset is so important as well. As the business grows the advisor will need to make decisions around culling clients, adding team members, and reducing securities positions. They will need to determine client profitability and service strategies by segment. They will need to work "on the business" as well as "in the business".

The Oechsli Institute has discovered 14 criteria affluent clients look for in advisors. The criteria are divided into two areas: communication and financial.

Communication expectations:
- Listen to them and understanding their family
- Be trustworthy
- Have deep industry knowledge
- Be a problem solver
- Provide personal communication

- Oversee the family's finances

Financial expectations:
- Meet investment expectations
- Seek to protect investments from downside
- Be transparent about fees
- Help create a financial plan
- Use current technology
- Coordinate their financial documents
- Provide insurance solutions

The "Ideal" Client

So, now that we have defined what clients want in their advisor let's talk about what the ideal client looks like and how as an advisor do you differentiate your practice?

First, I would suggest that the ideal client is one who has a certain level of investable assets and/or a certain level of disposable income. It is really hard to help someone who has no money nor the prospect of having any money. Whether you want to set a threshold and how much that may be is totally up to you and your firm. Secondly, clients must be open to your ideas and suggestions. By definition, if they want an advisor, they are likely advice seekers. Finally, they should be people you like working with. I know from experience how difficult and stressful it is to work with a client you don't connect with or don't like. You don't want to return their calls. You don't really want to meet with them. If you have some of these clients today, I would suggest you make arrangements to introduce them to another advisor that may be a better fit. They deserve that and they are not helping you. I found that I could adapt my style to many different personality styles, but I always struggled to connect with and work with analytical people. In retrospect, I should have introduced them to a colleague who may have been a better fit.

Here are a few ideas on how to differentiate yourself in the marketplace. **Specialize and niche down.** Instead of trying to be all things to all people, make a name for yourself as the advisor who specializes in working with doctors, or other professionals. Become the advisor who focuses on helping small business people. Get to be known as the advisor to see if you are an engineer. You get the idea. Get to know everything there is to know about your niche market. Learn to speak their language and start traveling in the circles they travel in. Hang out where they hang out – whether that's the golf club, the local Rotary Club, or the symphony society. You need to be careful here. Choose a niche that you enjoy working with and perhaps have already had some success connecting with. Make sure you can gain access to this market. I wouldn't suggest you target doctors if you have no connections, no way to get in front of them, or no desire to work with them.

In general, I didn't enjoy working with engineers. They can be nice people and some of my best friends are engineers. But they tend to be analytical by nature and want to study everything to death before they make a decision. That's just not me. I was taught to sell to this group by providing them with all kinds of data. I tried that but it was still difficult for me to make a connection. I was far more comfortable dealing with small business people. They were busy. They were used to taking advice from other professionals like their lawyers and accountants, and they made decisions relatively quickly. I learned to speak their language and we traveled in the same circles.

You can differentiate your practice in other ways too. You may choose to specialize in estate planning or insurance. You can become so expert in these areas and build such a positive reputation that clients seek you out. Perhaps accountants and lawyers will recommend you to their clients.

You may even become a portfolio manager and build your practice with clients that are looking for discretionary management of their money. Or you could buck the current trend and become known for your selection and recommendation of individual stocks and bonds.

The point here is that to be really successful you need to figure out what your target market is going to be.

In the early years, you may need to take on some clients that don't conform to your ideal client profile. You need to pay the bills, too. But I would strongly suggest that you resist the urge to take on any and everybody as clients. Otherwise, you will wind up with a hodgepodge book of clients, some of whom are extremely difficult to work with and hard to manage.

The same is true around how you plan to "run the money". Although there is more to wealth management than just managing investments, investment management is a key cornerstone of most financial plans. If you are a firm proponent of managed money, I would resist building your book with clients that are looking for advice on individual securities or commodities. Don't try to be all things to all people. It's impossible! Try instead to be all things to some people.

Let's put things in perspective. I would suggest that a nice practice today would have 150 clients with an average of $1 million in assets under management or administration. That practice should generate somewhere between $750,000 and $ 1.5 million in gross revenue. You don't need 1000 clients to make a good living. However, it may take a few years to get your business to where you want it and you need to grow your business one client at a time. Like most successful advisors, you will need to cull your book from time to time. **You will need to constantly be prospecting for new clients.** Even established advisors have clients who die or move away. God forbid, you or your firm may slip up or do something that results in a client leaving.

The Value Proposition

Clients today want to work with advisors who they are comfortable with and who provide value to them. I think an advisor needs to be able to succinctly communicate to the client or prospective client three things:

1) Who they are
2) What they do
3) What's in it for them

Although I have seen advisors who are successful in communicating their value proposition up front in the first meeting or even over the phone, I prefer the approach that starts first with a **focus on the client and what's important to them.** Too often I have seen advisors who think that their job is to tell the prospective client how great they are and how big and powerful their firm is. They then go on to tell the client what they do to provide value before they even know what the client is looking for.

I feel a far more impactful approach is to start by getting to know the prospective client. Find out who THEY are, who else is important to them, and what's important about money to them. After you know that and have confirmed with the client that you have heard them correctly, you can now talk about who you are, what you do, and how you can help them solve a problem or reach a financial goal.

You can differentiate your practice by really focusing on the client and listening to what they are saying.

We all know intuitively that it makes sense to ask questions and to listen to what our clients are telling us. Why then do so many advisors struggle with this? Why do they talk too much?

Some may not be aware that they are doing most of the talking. Some may think that is their job. Some may be anxious, and it just feels better to talk. Self-awareness and self-control are a big part of the solution. It also takes practice. I would suggest that every advisor video record a prospect and a client meeting and then critically examine who does most of the talking.

The First Meeting

Getting a prospect to agree to meet is a process and it can take time. It may follow a process that leads to "mini-wins". We will discuss prospecting and marketing a little later and in more depth.

To me, the first meeting with a prospective client is critical to success.

This is where the advisor needs to be on top of their game. But with practice, it can be fun.

Most advisors have it backward. As I stated earlier, they tend to open the meeting by telling the prospect all about themselves and their firm. I want to credit Bill Bachrach with teaching me a different approach.

Bill taught me to start the first meeting by focusing on the client; who they are, and what is important to them about money. By focusing on what was important about money to the prospect and determining the emotional connection that clients had with their money, I was able to quickly build a trusting relationship with them. I learned things that in some cases they had never shared with anyone else –

including their spouse! This led to a very close and trusted relationship with these clients. After asking questions about the importance of money to them and going deeper and deeper, I was then able to summarize and ask,

"Suppose I was able to come up with a plan that would help you to achieve x, y, and z, would we then have a basis for working together?"

This question is key. In sales parlance, it is known as a trial close/tie down. In a direct but soft way, it allowed me as an advisor to gauge where the clients were at in the sales process and whether we were likely to do business together. This was important before I launched into several hours of work preparing a financial plan.

If the answer to this question was "yes" then I would proceed to say "Great. Now I need to find out a little more about your current financial situation. Let's start by reviewing your assets". I would then launch into financial discovery and prepare a net worth statement and an income statement and find out whether they had valid wills in place, etc. I had prepared and sent out an agenda for the meeting in advance and asked them to bring their financial documents to the meeting. Nine times out of ten they did so it made information gathering much easier.

Finally, I would set up a date, time, and place for the second meeting where I would present the plan or recommendations. I am a huge proponent of using agendas for all meetings - especially client meetings.

Clients should know what the purpose of the meeting is, and the advisor should have an objective for each meeting. The agenda should be sent to the client in advance and they should have an opportunity to contribute to the agenda.

After pleasantries are exchanged at the beginning of the meeting, I recommend advisors check again with the client as to what is on their mind. You don't want to charge into your agenda only to find out 20 minutes later that the client is stuck on an issue or has something else on their mind. Check with them early and check often is a good axiom.

There are a few things that should happen at the first of every meeting. The advisor should check that the clients have adequate time to meet. "Do you have an hour or so?" was what I was taught to ask. The advisor should ensure that all the decision makers are present. This is very important and ignored all too often. Finally, the advisor should ask if there is anything the client wants to add to the agenda. If not, the advisor can briefly review what they have planned. In my mind, a productive client meeting should run for about an hour. Less is better but today advisors typically have a lot to cover in each meeting. Meetings should not last more than 90 minutes. If it's going to take more time than that, I would suggest scheduling a second meeting.

A big challenge to every meeting is to make them clear, concise, and to ensure that value is being added. It will be much easier to get agreement to meet again if the client comes away feeling like their time was respected and that they received value.

Finally, I would suggest that the advisor do a quick review of what was discussed and agreed to, and who is responsible for doing what before the next meeting. I would recommend that the topic, date, and time of the next meeting be agreed to before the client leaves the advisor's office. That way the meeting is in the calendar and there is no ambiguity about when they are meeting next and what will be discussed.

Soft Skills

Demonstrating empathy and connecting with the client on an emotional level is critical.

We all know someone who has been described as being able to "sell ice cubes to Eskimos". Being able to convince someone to take action on a solution that will help them is an admirable quality, and in fact, is part of good coaching. But selling someone something they don't need is not. Matt Oechsli says that "Today's affluent have become more jaded, more cynical, more skeptical than at any time in recent history, all of which makes this quality more significant. Empathy is the polar opposite of the slick value proposition, the grandiose claims or the marketing hype. It's a quality that engenders a level of trust that must be earned through one's actions. As an aside, the best salespeople have a high degree of empathy."

Top advisors and coaches ask questions and <u>listen actively.</u> They listen more than they talk. They focus on the client and the client's needs. The conversation is about the client, not about the advisor. They pay attention to verbal and non-verbal cues and are curious about the issues of concern or interest to the client. They re-phrase what they hear and check that they have heard correctly. Here's an example: "Ms. Client. What I heard was that it is important for you to not have to worry about money when you retire. Is that correct?"

Assertiveness Skills
A valuable skill is being able to communicate in an assertive fashion. This is important whether you are a manager or an advisor. Frankly, I think assertiveness is an important life skill

that every parent should be teaching their children. I learned how to be assertive later in life than I would have liked. It's basically telling others **what you like and what you don't like, what you want and what you don't want, and what you need and what you don't need.** It allows you to stand up for yourself without having to be aggressive or violent. It is the antithesis of passivity. Assertiveness is telling someone else how you feel. It is recognizing that you own your feelings and are responsible for your own well-being.

"Mr. Prospect. In order to provide you with the best advice, I need to completely understand where you are at financially. That makes sense doesn't it?"

This is an example of an assertive statement followed by a question. If the client answers "yes" then you can proceed to financial discovery not fearing that you may be seen as prying or intruding.

Here's another example, this time in a conversation between the manager and the advisor:

"Ms. Advisor. I want you to record your next client meeting. That way, you can watch the video after the meeting and look for things you are doing well and areas you may want to improve. I can also watch the video and we can get together after and compare notes. How does that sound?" Two more examples of assertiveness in conversation:

Here are two final examples of assertiveness in action:

"Mr. Assistant. We talked about this last week. It makes me angry when you don't follow through on what you said you were going to do. Our client service suffers and that is not good for business. Do you understand?"

"Ms. Associate Advisor. I like how you asked questions in that client meeting. You really listened to what they said, and I could tell that the clients felt that you understood their situation".

Technical Skills

Understanding the financial planning process and producing a plan for clients is table stakes today – but not all advisors deliver a plan. It is true that some clients are only interested in the management of their investments and don't want a holistic plan. However, the best advisors in the financial services business follow the 6-step process and ensure that their clients have a financial plan in place. This plan goes beyond the core topic of investment management and may include risk management and insurance, estate planning, retirement planning, and cash flow planning. The effective advisor needs to be knowledgeable and conversant in all these areas. Clients expect that their advisor understands the tax rules that pertain to investment income and these are considered in their recommendations around asset location. They expect their advisor to help them create an asset mix that considers their time horizon and tolerance for risk but will allow them to achieve their goals.

Another skill that an advisor needs to have today is proficiency in financial planning software. Unless their firm (or the advisor themselves) employs someone whose job it is to produce financial plans for their clients, then the advisor needs to know how to do that. Regardless of who inputs the data and produces the plan, the advisor needs to know how to analyze the data and to come up with recommendations that will help the client achieve their goals. They need to be able to effectively deliver the plan to the client. They need to be able to explain complex financial concepts in understandable terms.

Before that, they need to know how to conduct an effective discovery process. Effective discovery is far more than just finding out what assets, liabilities, income sources, and expenses the clients have. It's more than just risk management and estate planning. What are their dreams, goals, and values? What do they want to accomplish? Do they want to travel? What about family members – do they have financial or other responsibilities for parents or children? What does retirement look like? What about charitable giving? Is that important to them? It's really finding out what is important about money to the client.

Process Skills

Once a financial plan or a module of that plan is in place then the advisor and their team need to have a process for review and update. They need to plan when they will next meet with that client and what the topic of discussion may be. For example, the investment plan may be implemented, and the client's money invested for them. Next may be a more in-depth discussion with a will and estate planning specialist. There may be the need for wills to be updated and for powers of attorney and health directives to be put in place. Perhaps there is a need for life insurance or disability insurance.

It is virtually impossible to implement all of a comprehensive financial plan in one sitting. The best advisors do that over time and together with the client. Priority is given to minimizing risk and maximizing return.

Every client is different so it is unrealistic to expect that every client will have a comprehensive financial plan in place. But there better be evidence in the file that the advisor has had a discussion with the client around the six core topics. Should the client not wish to discuss or implement one area (let's say protecting their dependents with life insurance) that's fine but it needs to be documented in the client file that the discussion took place, a recommendation was made, and the client declined.

The best advisors have repeatable processes in place to prepare for a meeting and for running the meeting. They also have a process of follow up to ensure that commitments are honored. They ensure that the clients know in advance when they will meet again and what the topic of discussion will be. Most advisors have access to some administrative help, and some have large teams. As the team gets bigger the need for process and structure becomes greater. Everyone on the team needs to know what their role is and what the priorities are. I like teams to have a 30-minute weekly team meeting and a 5-10 minute stand up meeting at the beginning or end of each day. The purpose of the stand-up meeting is to talk about what they are doing today or plan to do tomorrow and who is doing what. The purpose of the weekly meeting is to talk about how things are going, what the goals are, and what the focus should be for the following week.

The Sales Process
Diagram 1 – Overview of the Sales Process

The process depicted above is pretty straightforward and applies to any industry. During my time as an advisor with Investors Group, I learned the sales process inside and out. It was stressed in my training that it was important to recognize where the client was in the process at all times and to ensure that I was at the same point with them. For example, if the advisor is about to present a solution to a problem and the client is still wondering what the problem is, then it is unlikely that the client will move forward. Another example: if the advisor is asking for the business and the client is still unsure if they are comfortable working with that advisor, then the process will likely stall. Where the advisor leads the client through the sales process and checks and affirms the client's comfort and understanding at each stage, there is a strong likelihood that they will do business together.

The Financial Planning Process

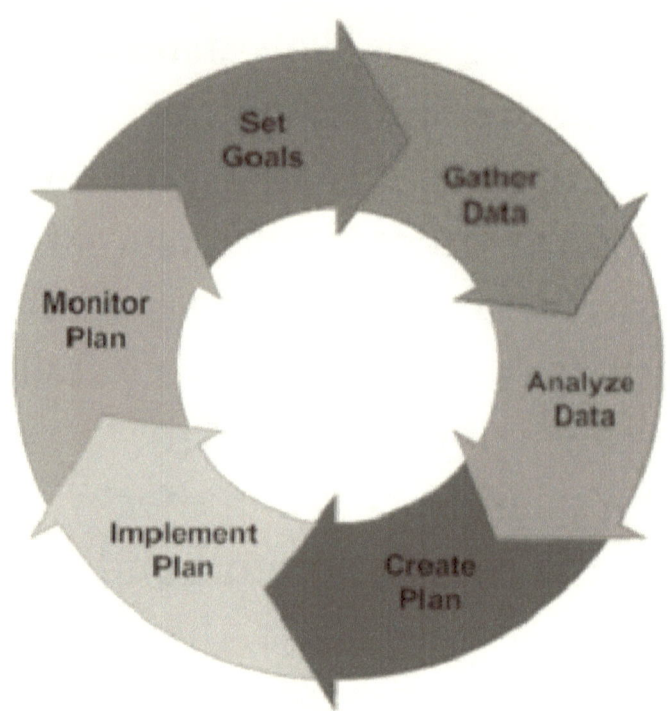

Diagram 2 - the Financial Planning Process

Diagram 2 above shows the Financial Planning Process. Many of the financial advisors I have worked with over the years hold the Certified Financial Planner (CFP) designation and I too received this designation in 1992. A condition of calling yourself a financial planner and using this designation requires you to follow the 6-step process depicted above. The Implementation phase (Step 5 of the financial planning process) corresponds directly to the "sale" or Step 6 of the Sales Process as depicted in Diagram 1.

We would argue that if the advisor does a good job of determining what is important to the client, and that if they are able to demonstrate that the solution they are proposing solves the problem the client is facing, then the close should be the natural conclusion to the discussion. No fancy closing technique is required nor does undue pressure need to be applied. For example, the advisor might say "Mrs. Client, do you see how what I am proposing will help you defer income tax today while helping you to save for retirement?" If the answer is yes, they can continue by asking "would you like to go ahead with what I am recommending?" That's it. It's simple. The key is asking great questions and active listening to determine what the client wants and needs.

The advisor then analyzes the situation and then prepares a financial plan including recommendations for implementation. If the client chooses to fulfill the recommendations with that advisor, this is when the sale of financial products takes place. So, the financial plan and the sales process are interwoven. At the end of the day, if the client decides to implement some or all the advisor's recommendations, then they have taken the next step toward achieving their goals. So, a "sale" is a good thing when what is proposed or being sold helps solve the client's problem, is presented openly and honestly, and is in their best interest. The fact that the advisor and their firm also benefit is okay too. That's what capitalism is and should be all about.

The best financial plan that does not get implemented does not benefit anyone, most importantly not the client.
From the time a financial advisor meets with a prospect for the first time until a "sale" is made can take more than one meeting. It may take as many as three meetings or more. The sales process can be complicated and require the use of sophisticated software and other resources to produce a financial plan. So, this is where the financial services industry may differ from other industries that have a simpler tangible product and

a shorter sales cycle. Nonetheless, top advisors understand the sales process.

Financial Planning

Most clients today want a financial plan. What constitutes a plan in their mind can vary from client to client. Not all clients want a comprehensive plan; that is a plan that addresses Investment Planning, Retirement Planning, Risk Management, Estate Planning, Tax Planning, and Cash Flow.

However, to help bulletproof your practice, I think you need to be prepared to discuss all six. If you are a Certified Financial Planner and you are not following the financial planning process and addressing these six components of a financial plan, then you are not practicing ethically according to the standards of your Financial Planning Standards Council.

I think all advisors should hold the CFP or be working toward that designation. It is the gold standard of our industry. Holding the CFP may no longer allow you to differentiate yourself from a competitor, but not holding the CFP can certainly put you at a disadvantage. You don't necessarily need to be the person on your team or in your branch office who is inputting the data into the software and actually producing the plan, but I think it is your responsibility as an advisor to ensure that you discuss each of these six areas with the client. For example, I think it is unconscionable for a financial advisor to not ensure that each client has a current will in place. This is even more important if they are married and have children.

Fiduciary Duty versus Duty of Care

There is a lot of discussion in the United States today about fiduciary duty and duty of care. In Canada, Registered Representatives have a duty of care to their clients. They are not fiduciaries. Fiduciaries must place their clients' interests ahead of their own. If we want to have the financial services industry recognized as a profession, I think this is the standard we need to aspire to. I think if clients understood the nuances of these definitions they would be surprised and perhaps shocked. I would guess that 99 out of 100 clients would think that their advisor puts the clients' interests ahead of their own interest or those of their firms. But advisors are not compelled to do so. This needs to change. The movement toward transparency of fees and the elimination of embedded commissions is a step forward. Countries such as Australia and the United Kingdom have passed legislation to eliminate embedded fees. "On Jan. 1, 2013, the UK regulator brought in Retail Distribution Review (RDR), aimed at ending commissions and replacing them with an up-front, fee-for-service model. At the same time, it raised the bar on minimum qualifications for advisors and set up "independent" and "restricted" advisors, outlining the kinds of products and services these advisors can or cannot sell." Susan Yellin – Investment and Insurance Journal – November 18, 2013.

Canada has not followed suit yet. The UK experience is interesting. According to Ms. Yellin, the number of advisors that have entered the industry has actually grown in recent years since the RDR was brought in. At the end of the day if we want our industry to be known as a profession, then professional standards need to be enhanced and potential conflicts of interest eliminated or at least drastically reduced. Firms in Canada are already moving to a fee for service model. Most offer fee-based accounts tied to assets under management. In most cases, this is a good model for clients and firms alike. Clients know how much they are paying and for what. Firms and advisors derive a more predictable level of revenue. I think the final move to a fiduciary relationship would actually be a positive one for the industry in Canada.

Building the Business

Unless you are an advisor with a bank or with a firm that provides you with a book of business, then this is job one. If you are starting from scratch and building the business one client at a time, then I hope you have an extensive list of contacts and connections that can become profitable clients or who can refer you to profitable prospects.

Most firms and most advisors have an expectation that their advisors will grow the business. This requires prospecting. When I was starting out as an advisor, I learned the importance of building in time for prospecting each week. As the business grew and I had more and more client meetings, it became important to look for ways to leverage existing relationships.

I think that every business needs a business plan and if we look at every advisor as running a small business, then it would hold that they should have a business plan too. A marketing plan or a business building plan should be part of that. Referrals are the lifeblood of an advisor's business. I have found that those advisors that have the three qualities we discussed above tend to become "referable". Many don't have to ask for referrals at all. Their clients are so enamored with them and they want their advisor to succeed. They refer friends and colleagues to them.

This doesn't usually happen overnight. In most cases, the advisor has worked long and hard to get to that point. So, what can advisors do to get new clients until that starts to happen for them?

Here are a few ideas that have worked for me and other advisors:

1) Ask for referrals – let your clients know you are open for business and describe the type of client you are looking for. Most people want to reciprocate. If they feel you have helped them, they will want to help you be successful.

2) Drip on prospects regularly using email – send articles that may be of interest to them. The goal is to add value and to eventually establish an online conversation. The next step after that is to take the online conversation offline. Next is to ask to meet for coffee,

lunch, or a game of golf. It is only after they feel that they know you that most prospects will agree to a business meeting. But if you don't ask you won't get.

3) Suppression of self-interest – reach out to prospects without looking for anything in return. Help them with something important to them. Send them an article that you saw that they may be interested in - business, gardening, sports, reading, etc.

4) Invite them to an event. I know when I am invited to see an NHL

game in a box I am pumped to go! What about tickets to the theater? What about a gift card to their favorite Starbucks, or a book on a topic of interest?

5) Social media – connect with business people and professionals on LinkedIn. Post articles on a regular basis and ask for feedback/opinion on a topic. Establish an online conversation. Again, the goal is to take an online conversation offline with the idea of eventually getting a meeting.

6) Invite them to a seminar. A great way for a prospect to see you in a

different light is for them to attend a seminar that you and colleagues are presenting. They can meet some of your other clients who hopefully will have nice things to say about you.

7) Digital Presence – ensure you have a website or that your personal page on your firm's website is up to date including a current picture. I would suggest employing a professional to help you create a webpage and strategies that sell and can drive traffic to your website while you sleep.

8) Blogs, posts, and other articles – write an article on a topic of interest to your niche market.

Share an article that you have read that you think may be of interest to your prospects or clients.

9) Webinars – I see more and more entrepreneurs using webinars as a means of connecting with prospects. Recently, I watched a webinar produced by a fellow coach who is looking to build their business. I also attended a webinar by Zoom on how to use webinars to build your business.

The more clients you have the more difficult it becomes to make time for prospecting. I am generally not a believer in multi-tasking but the ability to run a meeting with a client or even another prospect and at the same time get a referral to another prospect helped me to grow my business quickly.

Prospecting is essential to building a thriving practice. Clients die, they move away. You make a mistake, or your firm makes a mistake and the client moves to a competitor. So, unless you are cutting back or planning to retire or sell your business in the near future, you constantly need to be adding clients to your practice.

Prospecting can be intimidating for some advisors. Their underlying fear is usually that the prospect may not agree to meet and therefore that would validate the advisor's fear that they are a fraud, or not qualified, or flawed in some way. This negative self-talk leads to inaction (after all if you don't ask, they can't say no) but can also lead to self-loathing and a spiral of negative thoughts and feelings. The antithesis is positive self-talk and positive affirmation.

I have experienced all these thoughts and feelings myself. I learned to look at my fear objectively and to ask myself this question: **"What's the worst thing that could possibly happen"**. Typically, the answer is that "they won't become a client today". However, we tend to catastrophize and conclude that they don't like us, or that they reject us as a person, or that we will never be successful.

We are not suggesting "cold calling" as a business building strategy. What we are suggesting is that at some point you will need to ask the prospect if they would like to meet. Hopefully, this is after you have built a relationship online, offline, at a restaurant, or on the golf course. You have gotten to know them, and they have gotten to know you, and you **have already provided value.** After a series of "mini-wins" then it is much easier to ask the question.

This is no different than closing the sale. The close should be as easy as asking "would you like to go ahead with my suggestions?" or "would you like to meet to determine if we can be of help to you?".

Practice Management

I am a huge believer in setting goals and having a clear vision for a business. To me, a vision statement articulates what it will look like three or five years from now. It paints a picture and helps you to be clear on what you are working toward.

Goals can be shorter term and the collective achievement of your goals should allow you to move closer to realizing your vision. Action plans list the steps or activities that will get you to your goals. The raison d'etre of any business should be to earn a profit and a successful advisory practice should be no different. In addition to earning an above average income, I think every advisor should aspire to build a business that they can sell down the road.

So, I would suggest beginning with the end in mind.

If I were starting out today, I would want to build a business with 150 households with an average of $1 million in assets. I would be dually licensed as an RR and as a PM. I would have my CFP and would continue to complete courses in investment management leading to my CIM or even my CFA. I would have an assistant that would take care of administrative details and keep the trains running on time. I would only work with clients that I like and who take my advice. These clients would be business owners and professionals, people who I am comfortable relating to. I would take a holistic planning approach and utilize professional money managers for all but a relatively small group of clients and positions. I would ensure that my clients have an asset allocation that minimizes risk but allows them a reasonable chance of achieving their financial goals. I would focus on ensuring that they do not lose money. I would differentiate my practice by specializing and connecting with my clients on an emotional level. **I would ask good questions and actively listen.** I would take on an associate advisor when the business could afford it, and I would groom that person to take over my business when I want to retire or sell. I would work with a reputable firm that supports me and provides the back office and technology solutions that my team and my clients require.

Not every advisor shares the same vision and that's okay too. Like most things in life, some will not even have a vision. Many will not succeed. 80 % of the income will be earned by 20 % of the advisors.

In order to succeed and thrive today, I think advisors have to work hard, the need to work smart, and they need help along the way.

Building Trust

How do salespeople build trust and how can they build trust with a client quickly? As an advisor in the 1980s and 1990s, I found this to be a topic that was not given a lot of attention. We were trained to talk about what our firms did, how great they were, and how long they had been in business. We were encouraged to share how long we had been in business and the extensive training we had been through. We asked the clients about their goals and then tried to find solutions that would help them achieve their goals or overcome any obstacles in the way. We learned the difference between features and benefits, how to share these with the prospect, and how to ask for the business. Good, solid goals-based selling.

It was recognized that building a relationship with the client was critical to success and that it was important, to tell the truth, but it was generally accepted that building trust took time and was the result of ones' actions and not of ones' words. If you followed through on what you said you were going to do, that would build trust with the client. In other words, it was accepted that building trust takes time. But I wondered "if trust is the critical element of the relationship, and if the relationship is as important as the solution to winning business, how do we breach this gap and build trust quickly?"

The first time I was introduced to Bill Bachrach and **Values-Based Selling,** I knew I had found the answer. Although challenging to master, using Bill's values conversation helped me to take my personal advisory business to another level. By focusing on what was important about money to the prospect and determining the emotional connection that clients had with their money, I was able to quickly build a trusting relationship with them. I learned things that in some cases they had never shared with anyone else – including their spouse! This led to a very close and trusted relationship and tons of referrals.

Relationship Management

After the initial sale, there are usually subsequent topics for discussion and reasons to meet. Once the financial plan is completely "baked" it is important to keep in touch with clients. The frequency of contact is usually a combination of phone calls, emails, texts, virtual meetings, and in-person meetings. I would suggest that the plan needs to be reviewed and updated annually. Part of the review process should include an examination of whether the clients are on track to achieve their retirement and other investment goals. If not one of three things needs to happen. The clients need to lower their expectations or take more risk, or both.

Segmentation – after critical mass has been achieved, that is, the advisor's business is producing a sustainable level of revenue, it is important to segment the client base. This is done to identify the best clients and to determine appropriate service levels for each client. For example, "Gold clients" may expect two face to face meetings per year and a phone call every other month just to touch base. "Silver clients" might be entitled to one face to face and one virtual meeting per year and an outgoing phone call or email every quarter. "Bronze clients may expect one meeting per year and an email update every quarter.

You may argue that all clients regardless of assets under management or the revenue they drive should be entitled to the same level of service. That may be so in a perfect world, but we don't live in a perfect world. Also, most reasonable clients have a pretty good idea of where they are at on the pecking order, and what a reasonable level of service they might expect is. It is important for the advisor early in the process to ask the client what their expectations are in this regard. If your average client has $1 million invested with you then it is not likely that a client with $300,000 with you can expect to meet with you every month. Nor is this likely necessary.

The nice thing is that you as the advisor get to determine what you are able to commit to. I think more and more clients are open to virtual meetings and other forms of communication, but nothing replaces a face to face discussion.

Coaching

I have seen first-hand the impact that a good coach can have on an advisor. Before I became a coach of advisors and managers, I was a manager myself. I enjoyed the coaching component of leadership and that led me in this direction. Today, I coach a number of advisors. We talk about the business and the challenges that my advisors face, but we talk about so much more. These are husbands and wives, mothers and fathers, sons and daughters, and members of their respective communities. Their spouses have careers, too. They are under pressure to provide for and to raise and nurture their families. They have mortgages and car payments and want to provide for their children's education.

My "coachees" have problems and challenges. I help them to discover solutions to these problems. More importantly, I help them to learn how to solve their own problems. We all get "stuck" from time to time, and a coach can help you gain perspective and move past perceived and real obstacles.

Athletes and entertainers have employed coaches for many years. More recently, business leaders, entrepreneurs, and professionals have discovered the power of coaching. The first time I watched my coach trainer in a coaching session I was amazed. Although she is very experienced and skilled as a coach, I could not believe how she could help someone in the financial services business solve a problem, when she knows little about our business. I learned that she didn't need to. The power of coaching lies in the ability to ask the right questions at the right time, not in having all the answers. In most cases, the coachee has the answers. They just need help defining the problem and unlocking the solution.

So, if you currently don't have a coach, I would suggest you find one. I am partial to coaches who have professional training and are accredited by the International Coaching Federation (ICF). The ICF is the gold standard when it comes to coaching just like the CFP is now recognized universally as representing proficiency in financial planning. All accredited coaches have had formal training, audits of their practical coaching sessions, and have passed exams.

Peer coaching can be powerful too. Advisors can learn from one another and watching a colleague in action can be very impactful. They can ask to join a client meeting with a peer, or they may be able to watch a video of an actual meeting. In my opinion, video is under-utilized today.

Video Coaching

Video allows advisors to see themselves in action. They are able to see the good things they are doing in meetings and also identify areas for improvement. In 2015 when I was the national lead of coaching at MD Financial Management, we partnered with CMG Canada to provide video capability. This allowed advisors and their managers to watch their meetings. This is so powerful. As an advisor you and your manager can look at your data – number of contacts, number of meetings per week, revenue, etc. and draw certain conclusions. But data doesn't tell the whole story. What you see in a video (or in person) is how the advisor runs the meeting, how they interact and connect with the client, and what the client's reactions are. It's one thing to have someone (your manager or coach) comment on what they see. It's another to see for yourself.

I credit ATB Financial in Alberta for being a real leader in this area. They have a team of qualified coaches who watch videos of their financial advisors. Mastery moments are shared, and advisors are able to see the best practices in client engagement.

Entrepreneurial Approach to Time Management

I was fortunate in that a colleague and friend started attending Strategic Coach in the early 1990s. Tom shared with me one of the things that he learned, and that was the Strategic Coach Approach to Time Management.

Essentially, Dan Sullivan and his team believe that an entrepreneur needs to be rested and relaxed before they focus on key results areas of their business. "Free time" to them just that. It is time set aside to rejuvenate and recreate and includes no thoughts or actions pertaining to the business. This could be vacation time or just a day off at the beach. No work, no business planning, no business talk or calls.

"Focus time" revolves around the activities that result in revenue or decisions. For an investment advisor, I would suggest this is the time they spend face to face with or on the phone with clients. It can include active prospecting activities that the advisor is directly involved in.

Finally, "buffer time" is time for everything else. It is used for all the activities to prepare or follow up on focus time. As a financial advisor buffer time to me is the time spent preparing for a client meeting, preparing a financial plan, entering meeting notes in your CRM. Things of that nature.

Warren Buffett has only three or four engagements in his calendar each month. He wants to have time to read, to study and to think. The only thing he can't buy is time, so he guards it jealously. Bill Gates used to pack his days full of activities but has learned from Mr. Buffett that this is not necessarily the recipe for success or a happy life.

The first thing that goes into my calendar each week is my free time and the activities I like to do like playing golf, cycling, or hiking. Vacations and days off are blocked and time with family is prioritized. Next, I book time for focused activities like meeting with clients and prospecting. Finally, I book my buffer time for meeting preparation and follow up.

Tid Bits

Focus on doing one thing at a time and doing it well. Try to touch a piece of paper only once. Schedule time twice a day to read and reply to emails. Confirm all meetings and appointments

Mental Health - Managing Stress and Anxiety

As I discussed early in this book I see and talk with a lot of stressed-out advisors today. Stress is nature's way of telling us we need to take action. Stress in and of itself is not bad. Psychologists tell us that stress can help us to get things done. How we respond to stress is the key. If we respond negatively then we experience "distress". If we respond positively it is called "use stress".

A little bit of stress is good. Too much stress is not. It can get us out of bed in the morning and helps provide the energy to take action. I think about public speaking as a stressor. Organizations like Dale Carnegie use public speaking as a tool and a stressor to help people grow. Most great speakers feel a little nervous before they take to the stage. That energy, if channeled positively, can help them to deliver an inspiring talk. Today, if I am not a little nervous before I speak to a group then that makes me nervous!! I know there is a strong possibility I may be flat.

Why is it then that an activity like public speaking is feared and avoided by so many?

I believe it is fear and worry (anxiety). These feelings can be foreign and uncomfortable for many, so they avoid situations and opportunities that make them feel anxious. This deprives them of opportunities to make an impact and to succeed. They pass up opportunities to speak in front of a group of prospects or to ask for a meeting. They shy away from asking for the business.

A little bit of anxiety is normal. When it takes over or impedes how we live our lives it becomes a disorder. I know this because I have struggled with an anxiety disorder for most of my adult life. The good news is that I got professional help many years ago and that I have succeeded in spite of the disorder. In fact, I think the fact that I had to work hard to understand what made me feel the way I did has helped me to be a better coach today. I am in closer touch with own feelings. I learned strategies to help diffuse my own anxiety. I am able to relate to others who have suffered in this and other ways, and I'm able to provide direction to those who may struggle to manage their emotions.

How does this apply to a financial advisor? Learning to accept and face fear can help an advisor cope with stress. I have learned that fear becomes a coward when faced with just a small amount of courage. Unfortunately, the opposite is true. I have also learned that when I have given in to fear in the past, it grew in its power over me.

We all know that worrying is unproductive yet many of us engage in excessive worry. I learned to counter worry by being aware of my behavior and clearing my mind of my worries through daily diarizing. I now try to focus on more positive activities such as planning and acting.

Early in my advisory career, I worked with another advisor who would not make an outgoing prospecting call until his script was "perfect". He spent an inordinate amount of time crafting and practicing his script. This was in the days when we all made "cold calls". I suspect the real issue was fear of rejection on his part. Sadly, he couldn't force himself to pick up the phone and he was out of the business a month later.

It is not the case that top performers have only positive thoughts and feelings. They have good and bad days. They experience anxiety too. They just don't let it stop them from doing the things that most other people won't. They have learned to cope with stress. They live within their means. They minimize debt. They set reasonable targets. They face their fears. They manage their time and priorities effectively. They are disciplined They eat a balanced diet and get enough sleep. They exercise regularly. They don't try to do too much each day. They control their own calendar. They say "no" to requests that don't take them toward achieving their goals. They are assertive but not aggressive. They make mistakes, learn from them, and try not to repeat them. They are humble. They are always trying to get better so that they can be better for their clients, their families, and their firms. They are not afraid to ask for help.

Conclusion

The job of an investment advisor, financial advisor, financial planner, financial consultant, wealth manager, or whatever you want to call it has evolved over time. Some advisors continue to just talk about and advise their clients on investments, but most now provide holistic advice and add more value in doing so. It was a demanding occupation when I started out in 1983, and I think it is far more difficult today. Clients expect more, competition is fierce, firms expect more from their advisors, and regulations and regulators are more pervasive. The biggest challenge most new advisors have today is how to differentiate themselves. They must be able to answer the question "why should I do business with you?"

Advisors need to be able to build a business and to run it in a profitable manner. They need to manage their time and priorities so that the business supports their lives and not the other way around. They need to be energetic, enthusiastic, and resilient. They need to provide excellent client service and to listen to what their clients are saying. They need to be organized and supported by a solid team. They need to be able to communicate effectively. They need to be technically proficient. Finally, I believe an effective advisor needs the help of others, including a coach. It is a simple business, but it is not easy. Having a good coach can help an advisor sort through problems and overcome obstacles on their journey to excellence.

This is a difficult role and should continue to command an above average level of compensation. It can also be an extremely rewarding occupation. Advisors build great relationships with successful people in all walks of life. They have an opportunity to make significant contributions to the communities in which they live and work and to provide an above average standard of living for their families. My hope is that some of the ideas and strategies we have shared in this book will help an advisor in this process, and help them to build a bulletproof practice.

www.ingramcontent.com/pod-product-compliance
Lightning Source LLC
Chambersburg PA
CBHW031924170526
45157CB00008B/3043